LITERARY AWARDS WHO'S WHO

Dr. SUBHASSHRI. R

ISBN 979-8-89133-418-2

Dedicated to my Amma…

*who made me an insatiable trivia-collector to know ALWAYS
something more*

Preface

Just as a curious learner of literature, I had always innate interest in knowing the winners of several literary awards and their prize-winning oeuvres. Although now we have technology at our beck and call and a deluge of information is available at the click of button, I used to painstakingly note down and compartmentalize the information I collected during my high school days. As the popular saying goes, "Information is wealth" I always found collecting information made me a step ahead of my peers which made me earn me a funny title "fact-freak".

Probably this facet of collecting information ultimately landed me as a systematic researcher during my doctoral days and made me more and more inquisitive to learn stuffs with zest. At the same time, I find this book would be an ideal and handy to know more about the stellar writers who were bestowed with these prizes. In short, this book would be a one-stop for learners of literature who wish a quick revision before taking up any (literary) competitive examinations. I wish the possessor of the book to achieve excellence and come out in flying colours in their endeavors.

I acknowledge my grandparents' choicest blessings and their tales of wisdom which often enlighten my parched mind. My gratitude also goes to my parents who made me the habit of writing down anything interesting I come across. My super thanks to the pranks and antics of my siblings who tolerated my bickering and above all I warmly thank and acknowledge my quizmaster SMK of The Siol Quiz Club who taught me the art of taking points and making them remember for life. My special thanks to my students who see me as their favorite 'library akka'.

Contents

Jnanpith Award and its Awardees

Instituted in 1961, the Jnanpith Award is the highest literary award in India, presented annually for the best creative literary writing to writers belonging to any of the twenty-two scheduled languages, including English, recognised by the Indian constitution. The first award was presented in 1965 and from 1982 onwards, it was presented to a writer's overall contribution to literature, rather to a specific work. The award is sponsored by Bharatiya Jnanpith, a cultural organization, comprising of a cash award with a citation and a bronze replica of Vagdevi (Goddess Saraswathi), the Hindu goddess of learning.

Sl.no	Recipient	Language	Year
1.	G. Sankara Kurup	Malayalam	1965
2.	Tarasankar Bandyopadhyay	Bengali	1966
3.	Umashankar Joshi	Gujarati	1967
4.	Kuppali Venkatappa Puttappa 'Kuvempu"	Kannada	1967
5.	Sumitranandan Pant	Hindi	1968
6.	Firaq Gorakpuri	Urdu	1969

Sl.no	Recipient	Language	Year
7.	Viswanatha Satyanarayana	Telugu	1970
8.	Bishnu Dey	Bengali	1971
9.	Ramdhari Singh 'Dinkar'	Hindi	1972
10.	D.R. Bendre	Kannada	1973
11.	Gopinath Mohanty	Odia	1973
12.	Vishnu Sakharam Khandekar	Marathi	1974
13.	Akilan	Tamil	1975
14.	Ashapoorna Devi	Bengali	1976
15.	K. Shivaram Karanth	Kannada	1977
16.	Sachchidananda Vatsyayan	Hindi	1978
17.	Birendra Kumar Bhattacharya	Assamese	1979
18.	S.K. Pottekkatt	Malayalam	1980
19.	Amrita Pritam	Punjabi	1981
20.	Mahadevi Verma	Hindi	1982
21.	Masti Venkatesha Iyengar	Kannada	1983
22.	Thakazhi Sivasankara Pillai	Malayalam	1984
23.	Pannalal Patel	Gujarati	1985

Sl.no	Recipient	Language	Year
24.	Sachidananda Routray	Odia	1986
25.	Vishnu Vaman Shirwadhar "Kusumagraj"	Marathi	1987
26.	C. Narayana Reddy	Telugu	1988
27.	Qurratulain Hyder	Urdu	1989
28.	Vinayaka Krishna Gokak	Kannada	1990
29.	Subhash Mukhopadhyay	Bengali	1991
30.	Naresh Mehta	Hindi	1992
31.	Sitakant Mahapatra	Odia	1993
32.	U.R. Ananthamurthy	Kannad	1994
33.	M.T. Vasudevan Nair	Malayalam	1995
34.	Mahasweta Devi	Bengali	1996
35.	Ali Sardar Jafri	Urdu	1997
36.	Girish Karnad	Kannada	1998
37.	Nirmal Verma	Hindi	1999
38.	Gurdial Singh	Punjabi	1999
39.	Mamoni Raisom Goswami	Assamese	2000
40.	Rajendra Shah	Gujarati	2001

Sl.no	Recipient	Language	Year
41.	Jayakanthan	Tamil	2002
42.	Vinda Karandikar	Marathi	2003
43.	Rehman Rahi	Kashmiri	2004
44.	Kunwar Narayan	Hindi	2005
45.	Ravindra Kelekar	Konkani	2006
46.	Satya Vrat Shastri	Sanskrit	2006
47.	O.N.V. Kurup	Malayalam	2007
48.	Akhlaq Mohammed Khan "Shahryr"	Urdu	2008
49.	Amarkant	Hindi	2009
50.	Sri Lal Sukla	Hindi	2009
51.	Chandrshekhara Kambara	Kanada	2010
52.	Pratibha Ray	Odia	2011
53.	Ravuri Bharadhwaja	Telugu	2012
54.	Kedarnath Singh	Hindi	2013
55.	Bhalchandra Nemade	Marathi	2014
56.	Raghuveer Chaudhari	Gujarati	2015
57.	Shankha Ghosh	Bengali	2016

Sl.no	Recipient	Language	Year
58.	Krishna Sobti	Hindi	2017
59.	Amitav Ghosh	English	2018
60.	Akkitham Achuthan Namboothiri	Malayalam	2019
61.	Nilmani Phookan Jr	Assamese	2020
62.	Damodar Mauzo	Konkani	2021
63.	Nilamani Phookan	Assamese	2022

List of Moortidevi Award Winners

Although instituted in 1961, Moortidevi Award was first presented in 1983 by the Bharatiya Jnanpith. It is awarded only to Indian writers writing in Indian languages and the English language mentioned in Eight schedule of the Constitution of India with no posthumous conferral or self-nomination. However, from 2003 onwards, the award was given to authors for their "contemplation and perceptive work" (web) (Moortidevi Award) and consists of a cash prize of Rs. 1 lakh, a citation plaque, a shawl and a statue of Saraswati, the Hindu goddess of Leaning and wisdom.

Sl.no	Recipient	Work	Language	Year
1.	C.K. Nagaraja Rao	*Pattamahadevi Shantala Devi*	Kannada	1983
2.	Virendra Kumar Sakhlecha	-	Hindi	1984
3.	Kanhaiyalal Sethia	-	Rajasthani	1986
4.	Manubhai Pancholi	*Zer To Pidha Chhe Jani Jani*	Gujarati	1987
5.	Vishnu Prabhakar	-	Hindi	1988
6.	Vidya Niwas Mishra	-	Hindi	1989
7.	Munishree Nagraj	-	Hindi	1990
8.	Pratibha Ray	*Yagnaseni*	Odia	1991
9.	Kuber Nath Rai	-	Hindi	1992
10.	Shyamcharan Dubey	-	Hindi	1993

Sl.no	Recipient	Work	Language	Year
11.	Shivaji Sawant	*Mrityunjay*	Marathi	1994
12.	Nirmal Verma	*Bharat aur Europe: Pratishruti ke Shetra*	Hindi	1995
13.	Govind Chandra Pande	*Sahitya Saundarya aur Sanskriti*	Hindi	2000
14.	Rammurti Tripati	*Shriguru Mahima*	Hindi	2001
15.	Yashdev Shalya	-	Hindi	2002
16.	Kalyan Mal Lodha	-	Hindi	2003
17.	Narayan Desai	*Maroon Jeevan Aaj Mari Vaani*	Gujarati	2004
18.	Ram Murti Sharma	*Bharatiya Darshan Ki Chintadhara*	Hindi	2005
19.	Kishna Bihari Mishra	*Kalpataru Ke Utsav Leela*	Hindi	2006

Sl.no	Recipient	Work	Language	Year
20.	Veerappa Moily	*Shri Ramayana Mahaveshnam*	Kannada	2007
21.	Raghuvansh	*Paschimi Bhautik Samskriti Ka Utthan Aur Patan*	Hindi	2008
22.	Akkitham Achuthan Namboothiri	Various Poems	Malayalam	2009
23.	Gopi Chand Narang	*Urdu Ghazal aur Hindustani Zehn-o Tahzeeb*	Urdu	2010
24.	Gulab Kothari	*Ahmev Radha, Ahmev Krishnah*	Hindi	2011
25.	Haraprasad Das	*Vamsha*	Odia	2012
26.	C. Radhakrishnan	*Theekkadal Katanhu Thirumadhuram*	Malayalam	2013
27.	Vishwanath Tripathi	*Vyomkesh Darvesh*	Hindi	2014

Sl.no	Recipient	Work	Language	Year
28.	Kolakaluri Enoch	*Ananta Jeevanam*	Telugu	2015
29.	M.P. Veerendra Kumar	*Hymavathabhoovil*	Malayalam	2016
30.	Joy Goswami	*Du Dondo Phowara Matro*	Bengali	2017
31.	Vishwanath Tiwari	*Asti Aur Bhavti*	Hindi	2019
32.	M P Veerendra Kumar	*Hymavathabhoovil*	Malayalam	2021

List of Sahitya Akademi Award in English Winners

Established in 1954, the Sahitya Akademi Award is a literary award, awarded to writers of the most outstanding books of literary merit published in any of the twenty-four major languages. It is recognised to be the second highest literary award in India. Annually twenty-four writers are awarded including English. They are awarded by Sahitya Akademi Institute. The award comprises of a plaque and a cash prize of Rs. One Lakh.

Sl.no	Recipient	Work	Genre	Year
1.	R. K. Narayan	*The Guide*	Novel	1960
2.	Raja Rao	*The Serpent and the Rope*	Novel	1964
3.	Verrier Elwin	*The Tribal World of Verrier Elwin*	Autobiography	1965
4.	Bhabani Bhattacharya	*Shadow From Ladakh*	Novel	1967
5.	Niharrajan Ray	*An Artist in Life*	Biography	1969
6.	Mulk Raj Anand	*Morning Face*	Novel	1971
7.	Nirad C. Chaudhuri	*Scholar Extraordinary*	Biography	1975
8.	Sarvepalli Gopal	*Jawaharlal Nehru*	Biography	1976
9.	Chaman Nahal	*Azadi*	Novel	1977
10.	Anita Desai	*Fire on the Mountain*	Novel	1978

Sl.no	Recipient	Work	Genre	Year
11.	Rama Mehta	*Inside the Haveli*	Novel	1979
12.	K.R. Srinivasa Iyengar	*On the Mother*	Biography	1980
13.	Jayanta Mahapatra	*Relationship*	Poetry	1981
14.	Arun Joshi	*The Last Labyrinth*	Novel	1982
15.	Nissim Ezekiel	*Latter-Day Psalms*	Poetry	1983
16.	Keki N. Daruwalla	*The Keeper of the Dead*	Poetry	1984
17.	Kamala Das	*Collected Poems*	Poetry	1985
18.	Nayantra Sahgal	*Rich Like US*	Novel	1986
19.	Shiv K. Kumar	*Trap Falls in the Sky*	Poetry	1987
20.	Vikram Seth	*The Golden Gate*	Novel	1988
21.	Amitav Ghosh	*The Shadow Lines*	Novel	1989

Sl.no	Recipient	Work	Genre	Year
22.	Shashi Despande	*That Long Silence*	Novel	1990
23.	Allan Sealy	*The Trotter-Nama*	Novel	1991
24.	Ruskin Bond	*Our Trees Still Grows in Dehra*	Novel	1992
25.	G.N. Devy	*After Amnesia*	Essays	1993
26.	DomMoraes	*Serendip*	Poetry	1994
27.	Sunetra Gupta	*Memories of Rain*	Novel	1996
28.	Mahesh Dattani	*Final Solutions and Other Plays*	Drama	1998
29.	A.K. Ramanujan	*The Collected Poems*	Poetry	1999
30.	Kiran Nagarkar	*Cuckold*	Novel	2000

Sl.no	Recipient	Work	Genre	Year
31.	Rajmohan Gandhi	*Rajaji: A Life*	Biography	2001
32.	Amit Chaudhuri	*A New World*	Novel	2002
33.	Meenakshi Mukherjee	*The Perishable Empire*	Essays	2003
34.	Upamanyu Chatterjee	*The Mammaries of the Welfare State*	Novel	2004
35.	Arundathi Roy	*The Algebra of Infinite Justice*	Essays	2005
36.	Rupa Bajwa	*The Sari Shop*	Novel	2006
37.	Malathi Rao	*Disorderly Women*	Novel	2007
38.	Chaturvedi Badrinath	*Mahabharata: An Inquiry into the Human Condition*	Criticism	2009
39.	Esther David	*The Book of Rachel*	Novel	2010

Sl.no	Recipient	Work	Genre	Year
40.	Ramachandra Guha	*India After Gandhi*	Historical Narrative	2011
41.	Jeet Thayil	*These Errors are Correct*	Poetry	2012
42.	Temsula Ao	*Laburnum For My Head*	Short Stories	2013
43.	Adil Jussawalla	*Trying to Say Goodbye*	Poetry	2014
44.	Cyrus Mistry	*Chronicle of a Corpse Bearer*	Novel	2015
45.	Jerry Pinto	*Em and the Big Hoom*	Novel	2016
46.	Mamang Dai	*The Black Hill*	Novel	2017
47.	Anees Salim	*The Blind Lady's Descendants*	Novel	2018
48.	Shashi Tharoor	*An Era of Darkness*	Novel (non-fiction)	2019

Sl.no	Recipient	Work	Genre	Year
49.	Arundhathi Subramaniam	*When God is a Traveller*	Poetry	2020
50.	Namita Gokhale	*Things to Leave Behind*	Novel	2021
51.	Anuradha Roy	*All The Lives We Never Lived*	Novel	2022

List of Nobel Prize For Literature Winners

Recognised to be one of the renowned literary awards globally, it was instituted in 1900 by the Swedish inventor cum industrialist – Alfred Nobel. According to Nobel's will, it is awarded "to those who, during the preceding year, shall have conferred by the greatest benefit on mankind" (Nobel Prize) in the field of literature. The first award was presented in 1901 and conferred by the Swedish Academy in Stockholm. Every year, during the month of October, the Academy announces the Nobel Laureate and it is one of the five Nobel prizes established by the will of Alfred Nobel in 1895.

Sl. no	Laureate's Name	Nationality	Genre	Remarks (if any)	Year awarded
1.	Sally Prudhomme	France	Poet	"in special recognition of his poetic composition, which gives evidence of lofty idealism, artistic perfection and a rare combination of the qualities of both heart and intellect"	1901
2.	Theodor Mommsen	Germany	Historian	"the greatest living master of the art of historical writing, with special reference to his monumental work, *A history of Rome*"	1902

Sl. no	Laureate's Name	Nationality	Genre	Remarks (if any)	Year awarded
3.	Bjornstjerne Martinius Bjornson	Norway	Novelist, Poet, Dramatist	"as a tribute to his noble, magnificent and versatile poetry, which has always been distinguished by both the freshness of its inspiration and the rare purity of its spirit"	1903
4.	Jose Echegaray y Eizaguirre	Spain	Dramatist	"in recognition of the numerous and brilliant compositions which, in an individual and original manner, have revived the great traditions of the Spanish drama"	1904

Sl. no	Laureate's Name	Nationality	Genre	Remarks (if any)	Year awarded
5.	Frederic Mistral	France	Poet	"in recognition of the fresh originality and true inspiration of his poetic production, which faithfully reflects the natural scenery and native spirit of his people, and, in addition, his significant work as a Provençal philologist"	1904
6.	Henryk Sienkiewicz	Poland	Novelist	"because of his outstanding merits as an epic writer"	1905

Sl. no	Laureate's Name	Nationality	Genre	Remarks (if any)	Year awarded
7.	Giousue Carducci	Italy	Poet	"not only in consideration of his deep learning and critical research, but above all as a tribute to the creative energy, freshness of style, and lyrical force which characterize his poetic masterpieces"	1906

Sl. no	Laureate's Name	Nationality	Genre	Remarks (if any)	Year awarded
8.	Rudyard Kipling	UK	Poet, Novelist	"in consideration of the power of observation, originality of imagination, virility of ideas and remarkable talent for narration which characterize the creations of this world-famous author"	1907

Sl. no	Laureate's Name	Nationality	Genre	Remarks (if any)	Year awarded
9.	Rudolf Christoph Eucken	Germany	Philosopher	"in recognition of his earnest search for truth, his penetrating power of thought, his wide range of vision, and the warmth and strength in presentation with which in his numerous works he has vindicated and developed an idealistic philosophy of life"	1908
10.	Selma Lagerlof	Sweden	Novelist	"in appreciation of the lofty idealism, vivid imagination and spiritual perception that characterize her writings"	1909

Sl. no	Laureate's Name	Nationality	Genre	Remarks (if any)	Year awarded
11.	Paul Johann Ludwig von Heyse	Germany	Poet, Novelist, Dramatist	"as a tribute to the consummate artistry, permeated with idealism, which he has demonstrated during his long productive career as a lyric poet, dramatist, novelist and writer of world-renowned short stories"	1910

Sl. no	Laureate's Name	Nationality	Genre	Remarks (if any)	Year awarded
12.	Maurice Maeterlinck	Belgium	Dramatist	"in appreciation of his many-sided literary activities, and especially of his dramatic works, which are distinguished by a wealth of imagination and by a poetic fancy, which reveals, sometimes in the guise of a fairy tale, a deep inspiration, while in a mysterious way they appeal to the readers' own feelings and stimulate their imaginations"	1911

Sl. no	Laureate's Name	Nationality	Genre	Remarks (if any)	Year awarded
13.	Gerhart Hauptmann	Germany	dramatist	"primarily in recognition of his fruitful, varied and outstanding production in the realm of dramatic art"	1912
14.	Rabindranath Tagore	India	Poet	"because of his profoundly sensitive, fresh and beautiful verse, by which, with consummate skill, he has made his poetic thought, expressed in his own English words, a part of the literature of the West"	1913

Sl. no	Laureate's Name	Nationality	Genre	Remarks (if any)	Year awarded
15.	Romain Rolland	France	Novelist	"as a tribute to the lofty idealism of his literary production and to the sympathy and love of truth with which he has described different types of human beings"	1915
16.	Verner von Heidenstam	Sweden	Poet	"in recognition of his significance as the leading representative of a new era in our literature"	1916
17.	Karl Gjelleup	Denmark	Novelist	"for his varied and rich poetry, which is inspired by lofty ideals"	1917

Sl. no	Laureate's Name	Nationality	Genre	Remarks (if any)	Year awarded
18.	Henrik Pontoppidan	Denmark	novelist	"for his authentic descriptions of present-day life in Denmark"	1917
19.	Erik Axel Karlfeldt (declined)	Sweden	Poet		1918
20.	Carl Spitteler	Switzerland	Poet, novelist	"in special appreciation of his epic, *Olympian Spring*"	1919
21.	Knut Hamsun	Norway	Novelist	"for his monumental work, *Growth of the Soil*"	1920

Sl. no	Laureate's Name	Nationality	Genre	Remarks (if any)	Year awarded
22.	Anatole France	France	Novelist	"in recognition of his brilliant literary achievements, characterized as they are by a nobility of style, a profound human sympathy, grace, and a true Gallic temperament"	1921
23.	Jacinto Benavente y Martinez	Spain	Dramatist	"for the happy manner in which he has continued the illustrious traditions of the Spanish drama"	1922

Sl. no	Laureate's Name	Nationality	Genre	Remarks (if any)	Year awarded
24.	William Butler Yeats	Ireland	Poet	"for his always inspired poetry, which in a highly artistic form gives expression to the spirit of a whole nation"	1923
25.	Wladyslaw Stainslaw Reymont	Poland	Novelist	"for his great national epic, *The Peasants*"	1924
26.	George Bernard Shaw	Ireland	Dramatist	"for his work which is marked by both idealism and humanity, its stimulating satire often being infused with a singular poetic beauty"	1925

Sl. no	Laureate's Name	Nationality	Genre	Remarks (if any)	Year awarded
27.	Grazia Deledda	Italy	Novelist	"for her idealistically inspired writings which with plastic clarity picture the life on her native island and with depth and sympathy deal with human problems in general"	1926
28.	Henri Bergson	France	Philosopher	"in recognition of his rich and vitalizing ideas and the brilliant skill with which they have been presented"	1927
29.	Sigrid Undset	Norway	Novelist	"principally for her powerful descriptions of Northern life during the Middle Ages"	1928

Sl. no	Laureate's Name	Nationality	Genre	Remarks (if any)	Year awarded
30.	Thomas Mann	Germany	Novelist	"principally for his great novel, *Buddenbrooks*, which has won steadily increased recognition as one of the classic works of contemporary literature"	1929
31.	Sinclair Lewis	United States	Novelist	"for his vigorous and graphic art of description and his ability to create, with wit and humour, new types of characters"	

Sl. no	Laureate's Name	Nationality	Genre	Remarks (if any)	Year awarded
32.	Erik Axel Karlfeldt (Posthumous Award)	Sweden	Poet	"The poetry of Erik Axel Karlfeldt"	1931
33.	John Galsworthy	UK	Novelist	"for his distinguished art of narration which takes its highest form in *The Forsyte Saga*"	1932
34.	Ivan Alekseyevich Bunin	USSR	Poet, novelsit	"for the strict artistry with which he has carried on the classical Russian traditions in prose writing"	1933

Sl. no	Laureate's Name	Nationality	Genre	Remarks (if any)	Year awarded
35.	Luigi Pirandello	Italy	Dramatist	"for his bold and ingenious revival of dramatic and scenic art"	1934
36.	Eugene o' Neill	United States	dramatist	"for the power, honesty and deep-felt emotions of his dramatic works, which embody an original concept of tragedy"	1936

Sl. no	Laureate's Name	Nationality	Genre	Remarks (if any)	Year awarded
37.	Roger Martin du Gard	France	Novelist	"for the artistic power and truth with which he has depicted human conflict as well as some fundamental aspects of contemporary life in his novel-cycle *Les Thibault*"	1937
38.	Pearl S. Buck	United States	Novelist	"for her rich and truly epic descriptions of peasant life in China and for her biographical masterpieces"	1938

Sl. no	Laureate's Name	Nationality	Genre	Remarks (if any)	Year awarded
39.	Frans Eemil Sillanpaa	Finland	Novelist	"for his deep understanding of his country's peasantry and the exquisite art with which he has portrayed their way of life and their relationship with Nature"	1939
40.	Johannes V. Jensen	Denmark	Novelist	"for the rare strength and fertility of his poetic imagination with which is combined an intellectual curiosity of wide scope and a bold, freshly creative style"	1944

Sl. no	Laureate's Name	Nationality	Genre	Remarks (if any)	Year awarded
41.	Gabriela Mistral	Chile	Poet	"for her lyric poetry which, inspired by powerful emotions, has made her name a symbol of the idealistic aspirations of the entire Latin American world"	1945
42.	Hermann Hesse	Switzerland	Novelist	"for his inspired writings which, while growing in boldness and penetration, exemplify the classical humanitarian ideals and high qualities of style"	1946

Sl. no	Laureate's Name	Nationality	Genre	Remarks (if any)	Year awarded
43.	Andre Gide	France	Novelist, Essayist	for his comprehensive and artistically significant writings, in which human problems and conditions have been presented with a fearless love of truth and keen psychological insight"	1947
44.	T.S. Eliot	UK	Poet, critic	"for his outstanding, pioneer contribution to present-day poetry"	1948
45.	William Faulkner	United States	Novelist	"for his powerful and artistically unique contribution to the modern American novel"	1949

Sl. no	Laureate's Name	Nationality	Genre	Remarks (if any)	Year awarded
46.	Betrand Russell	UK	Philosopher	"in recognition of his varied and significant writings in which he champions humanitarian ideals and freedom of thought"	1950
47.	Par Lagerkvist	Sweden	Novelist	"for the artistic vigour and true independence of mind with which he endeavours in his poetry to find answers to the eternal questions confronting mankind"	1951

Sl. no	Laureate's Name	Nationality	Genre	Remarks (if any)	Year awarded
48.	Francois Mauriac	France	Poet, Novelist, dramatist	"for the deep spiritual insight and the artistic intensity with which he has in his novels penetrated the drama of human life"	1952
49.	Sir Winston Churchill	UK	Historian, Orator	"for his mastery of historical and biographical description as well as for brilliant oratory in defending exalted human values"	1953

Sl. no	Laureate's Name	Nationality	Genre	Remarks (if any)	Year awarded
50.	Ernest Hemingway	United States	Novelist	"for his mastery of the art of narrative, most recently demonstrated in *The Old Man and the Sea,* and for the influence that he has exerted on contemporary style"	1954
51.	Halldor Laxness	Iceland	Novelist	"for his vivid epic power which has renewed the great narrative art of Iceland"	1955
52.	Juan Ramon Jimenez	Spain	Poet	"for his lyrical poetry, which in Spanish language constitutes an example of high spirit and artistical purity"	1956

Sl. no	Laureate's Name	Nationality	Genre	Remarks (if any)	Year awarded
53.	Albet Camus	France	Novelist, Dramatist	"for his important literary production, which with clear-sighted earnestness illuminates the problems of the human conscience in our times"	1957
54.	Boris Leonidovich Pasternak (declined)	USSR	Novelist, Poet	"for his important achievement both in contemporary lyrical poetry and in the field of the great Russian epic tradition"	1958

Sl. no	Laureate's Name	Nationality	Genre	Remarks (if any)	Year awarded
55.	Salvatore Quasimodo	Italy	Poet	"for his lyrical poetry, which with classical fire expresses the tragic experience of life in our own times"	1959
56.	Saint-John Perse	France	Poet	"for the soaring flight and the evocative imagery of his poetry which in a visionary fashion reflects the conditions of our time"	1960
57.	Ivo Andric	Yugoslavia	Novelist	"for the epic force with which he has traced themes and depicted human destinies drawn from the history of his country"	1961

Sl. no	Laureate's Name	Nationality	Genre	Remarks (if any)	Year awarded
58.	John Steinbeck	United States	Novelist	"for his realistic and imaginative writings, combining as they do sympathetic humour and keen social perception"	1962
59.	George Seferis	Greece	Poet	"for his eminent lyrical writing, inspired by a deep feeling for the Hellenic world of culture"	1963

Sl. no	Laureate's Name	Nationality	Genre	Remarks (if any)	Year awarded
60.	Jean Paul Satre (declined)	France	Philosopher, dramatist	"for his work which, rich in ideas and filled with the spirit of freedom and the quest for truth, has exerted a far-reaching influence on our age"	1964
61.	Mikhail Aleksandrovich Sholokhov	USSR	Novelist	"for the artistic power and integrity with which, in his epic of the Don, he has given expression to a historic phase in the life of the Russian people"	1965

Sl. no	Laureate's Name	Nationality	Genre	Remarks (if any)	Year awarded
62.	S. Y. Agnon	Israel	Novelist	"for his profoundly characteristic narrative art with motifs from the life of the Jewish people"	1966
63.	Nelly Sachs	Sweden	Poet	"for her outstanding lyrical and dramatic writing, which interprets Israel's destiny with touching strength"	1966
64.	Miguel Angel Asturias	Guatemala	Novelist	"for his vivid literary achievement, deep-rooted in the national traits and traditions of Indian peoples of Latin America"	1967

Sl. no	Laureate's Name	Nationality	Genre	Remarks (if any)	Year awarded
65.	Kawabat Yasunari	Japan	Novelist	"for his narrative mastery, which with great sensibility expresses the essence of the Japanese mind"	1968
66.	Samuel Beckett	Ireland	Novelist, dramatist	"for his writing, which – in new forms for the novel and drama – in the destitution of modern man acquires its elevation"	1969,
67.	Aleksandr Isayevich Solzhenitsyn	USSR	novelist	"for the ethical force with which he has pursued the indispensable traditions of Russian literature"	1970

Sl. no	Laureate's Name	Nationality	Genre	Remarks (if any)	Year awarded
68.	Pablo Neruda	Chile	Poet	"for a poetry that with the action of an elemental force brings alive a continent's destiny and dreams"	1971
69.	Heinrich Boll	West Germany	Novelist	"for his writing which through its combination of a broad perspective on his time and a sensitive skill in characterization has contributed to a renewal of German literature"	1972

Sl. no	Laureate's Name	Nationality	Genre	Remarks (if any)	Year awarded
70.	Patrick White	Australia	Novelist	"for an epic and psychological narrative art which has introduced a new continent into literature"	1973
71.	Eyvind Johnson	Sweden	Novelist, Poet	"for writings that catch the dewdrop and reflect the cosmos"	1974
72.	Harry Martinson	Sweden	Novelist, Poet	"for a narrative art, far-seeing in lands and ages, in the service of freedom"	1974

Sl. no	Laureate's Name	Nationality	Genre	Remarks (if any)	Year awarded
73.	Eugenio Montale	Italy	Poet	"for his distinctive poetry which, with great artistic sensitivity, has interpreted human values under the sign of an outlook on life with no illusions"	1975
74.	Saul Bellow	United States	Novelist	"for the human understanding and subtle analysis of contemporary culture that are combined in his work"	1976

Sl. no	Laureate's Name	Nationality	Genre	Remarks (if any)	Year awarded
75.	Vicente Alexiandre	Spain	Poet	"for a creative poetic writing which illuminates man's condition in the cosmos and in present-day society, at the same time representing the great renewal of the traditions of Spanish poetry between the wars"	1977
76.	Issac Bashevis Singer	United States	Novelist	"for his impassioned narrative art which, with roots in a Polish-Jewish cultural tradition, brings universal human conditions to life"	1978

Sl. no	Laureate's Name	Nationality	Genre	Remarks (if any)	Year awarded
77.	Odysseus Elytis	Greece	Poet	"for his poetry, which, against the background of Greek tradition, depicts with sensuous strength and intellectual clear-sightedness modern man's struggle for freedom and creativeness"	1979
78.	Czesław Miłosz	United States	Poet	"who with uncompromising clear-sightedness voices man's exposed condition in a world of severe conflicts"	1980
79.	Elias Canetti	Bulgaria	Novelist, essayist	"for writings marked by a broad outlook, a wealth of ideas and artistic power"	1981

Sl. no	Laureate's Name	Nationality	Genre	Remarks (if any)	Year awarded
80.	Gabriel Garcia Marquez	Colombia	Novelist, journalist, Social Critic	"for his novels and short stories, in which the fantastic and the realistic are combined in a richly composed world of imagination, reflecting a continent's life and conflicts"	1982
81.	Sir William Golding	UK	Novelist	"for his novels which, with the perspicuity of realistic narrative art and the diversity and universality of myth, illuminate the human condition in the world of today"	1983

Sl. no	Laureate's Name	Nationality	Genre	Remarks (if any)	Year awarded
82.	Jaroslav Seifert	Czechoslovakia	Poet	"for his poetry which endowed with freshness, sensuality and rich inventiveness provides a liberating image of the indomitable spirit and versatility of man"	1984
83.	Claude Simon	France	Novelist	"who in his novel combines the poet's and the painter's creativeness with a deepened awareness of time in the depiction of the human condition"	1985

Sl. no	Laureate's Name	Nationality	Genre	Remarks (if any)	Year awarded
84.	Wole Soyinka	Nigeria	Dramatist, Poet	"who in a wide cultural perspective and with poetic overtones fashions the drama of existence"	1986
85.	Joseph Brodsky	United States	Poet, Essayist	"for an all-embracing authorship, imbued with clarity of thought and poetic intensity"	1987
86.	Naguib Mahfouz	Egypt	Novelist	"who, through works rich in nuance – now clear-sightedly realistic, now evocatively ambiguous – has formed an Arabian narrative art that applies to all mankind"	1988

Sl. no	Laureate's Name	Nationality	Genre	Remarks (if any)	Year awarded
87.	Camilo Jose Cela	Spain	Novelist	"for a rich and intensive prose, which with restrained compassion forms a challenging vision of man's vulnerability"	1989
88.	Octavio Paz	Mexico	Poet, Essayist	"for impassioned writing with wide horizons, characterized by sensuous intelligence and humanistic integrity"	1990

Sl. no	Laureate's Name	Nationality	Genre	Remarks (if any)	Year awarded
89.	Nadine Gordimer	South Africa	Novelist	"who through her magnificent epic writing has – in the words of Alfred Nobel – been of very great benefit to humanity"	1991
90.	Derek Walcott	Saint Lucia	Poet	"for a poetic oeuvre of great luminosity, sustained by a historical vision, the outcome of a multicultural commitment"	1992

Sl. no	Laureate's Name	Nationality	Genre	Remarks (if any)	Year awarded
91.	Toni Morrison	United States	Novelist	"who in novels characterized by visionary force and poetic import, gives life to an essential aspect of American reality"	1993
92.	Oe Kenzaburo	Japan	Novelist	"who with poetic force creates an imagined world, where life and myth condense to form a disconcerting picture of the human predicament today"	1994

Sl. no	Laureate's Name	Nationality	Genre	Remarks (if any)	Year awarded
93.	Seamus Heaney	Ireland	Poet	"for works of lyrical beauty and ethical depth, which exalt everyday miracles and the living past"	1995
94.	Wislaw Szymborska	Poland	Poet	"for poetry that with ironic precision allows the historical and biological context to come to light in fragments of human reality"	1996
95.	Dario Fo	Italy	Dramatist, Actor	"who emulates the jesters of the Middle Ages in scourging authority and upholding the dignity of the downtrodden"	1997

Sl. no	Laureate's Name	Nationality	Genre	Remarks (if any)	Year awarded
96.	Jose Saramago	Portugal	Novelist	"who with parables sustained by imagination, compassion and irony continually enables us once again to apprehend an elusory reality"	1998
97.	Gunter Grass	Germany	Novelist	"whose frolicsome black fables portray the forgotten face of history"	1999
98.	Gao Xingjian	France	Novelist, dramatist	"for an æuvre of universal validity, bitter insights and linguistic ingenuity, which has opened new paths for the Chinese novel and drama"	2000

Sl. no	Laureate's Name	Nationality	Genre	Remarks (if any)	Year awarded
99.	Sir V.S. Naipaul	Trinidad	Novelist	"for having united perceptive narrative and incorruptible scrutiny in works that compel us to see the presence of suppressed histories"	2001
100.	Imre Kertesz	Hungary	Novelist	"for writing that upholds the fragile experience of the individual against the barbaric arbitrariness of history"	2002
101.	JM Coetzee	South Africa	Novelist	"who in innumerable guises portrays the surprising involvement of the outsider"	2003

Sl. no	Laureate's Name	Nationality	Genre	Remarks (if any)	Year awarded
102.	Elfriede Jelinek	Austria	Novelist, Dramatist	"for her musical flow of voices and counter-voices in novels and plays that with extraordinary linguistic zeal reveal the absurdity of society's clichés and their subjugating power"	2004
103.	Harold Pinter	UK	Dramatist	"who in his plays uncovers the precipice under everyday prattle and forces entry into oppression's closed rooms"	2005

Sl. no	Laureate's Name	Nationality	Genre	Remarks (if any)	Year awarded
104.	Orhan Pamuk	Turkey	Novelist	"who in the quest for the melancholic soul of his native city has discovered new symbols for the clash and interlacing of cultures"	2006
105.	Doris Lessing	UK	Novelist	"that epicist of the female experience, who with scepticism, fire and visionary power has subjected a divided civilisation to scrutiny"	2007

Sl. no	Laureate's Name	Nationality	Genre	Remarks (if any)	Year awarded
106.	Jean-Marie Gustave Le Clézio	France	Novelist, essayist	"author of new departures, poetic adventure and sensual ecstasy, explorer of a humanity beyond and below the reigning civilization"	2008
107.	Herta Muller	Germany	novelist	"who, with the concentration of poetry and the frankness of prose, depicts the landscape of the dispossessed"	2009

Sl. no	Laureate's Name	Nationality	Genre	Remarks (if any)	Year awarded
108.	Mario Vargas Llosa	Peru	Novelist, dramatist	"for his cartography of structures of power and his trenchant images of the individual's resistance, revolt, and defeat"	2010
109.	Tomas Transtromer	Sweden	poet	"because, through his condensed, translucent images, he gives us fresh access to reality"	2011
110.	Mo Yan	China	Novelist, short-story writer	"who with hallucinatory realism merges folk tales, history and the contemporary"	2012

Sl. no	Laureate's Name	Nationality	Genre	Remarks (if any)	Year awarded
111.	Alice Munro	Canada	Short-story writer	"master of the contemporary short story"	2013
112.	Patrick Modiano	France	novelist	"for the art of memory with which he has evoked the most ungraspable human destinies and uncovered the life-world of the occupation"	2014
113.	Svetlana Alexievich	Belarus	Journalist, Prose Writer	"for her polyphonic writings, a monument to suffering and courage in our time"	2015

Sl. no	Laureate's Name	Nationality	Genre	Remarks (if any)	Year awarded
114.	Bob Dylan	United States	Singer, Songwriter	"for having created new poetic expressions within the great American song tradition"	2016
115.	Kazue Oshiguro	UK	Novelist	"who, in novels of great emotional force, has uncovered the abyss beneath our illusory sense of connection with the world"	2017
116.	Olga Tokarczuk	Poland	Novelist, Poet, Essayist	"for a narrative imagination that with encyclopedic passion represents the crossing of boundaries as a form of life"	2018

Sl. no	Laureate's Name	Nationality	Genre	Remarks (if any)	Year awarded
117.	Peter Handke	Austria	Novelist, Poet, Essayist, Playwright	"for an influential work that with linguistic ingenuity has explored the periphery and the specificity of human experience"	2019
118.	Louise Gluck	United States	Poet	"for her unmistakable poetic voice that with austere beauty makes individual existence universal".	2020

Sl. no	Laureate's Name	Nationality	Genre	Remarks (if any)	Year awarded
119.	Abdulrazak Gurnah	Born in Zanzibar & active in England	Novelist	"for his uncompromising and compassionate penetration of the effects of colonialism and the fate of the refugee in the gulf between cultures and continents."	2021
120.	Annie Ernaux	France	Novelist	"for the courage and clinical acuity with which she uncovers the roots, estrangements and collective restraints of personal memory"	2022

List of Booker Prize Winners

Formerly known as Man Booker Prize, it was founded in 1969, the International Booker Prize was awarded to writers who "continued creativity, development and overall contribution to fiction on the world stage" (web). The process to winner begins once an advisory committee, which includes a writer, two publishers, a literary agent, a bookseller, a librarian, and a chairperson gets appointed by the foundation. The committee then selects a judging panel, which changes every year. The judges are selected from leading critics, writers and academics. The Booker Prize winner them is announced in an event in London's Guildhall in October.

Sl.no	Winner	Novel	Country	Year
1.	P. H. Newby	*Something to Answer For*	United Kingdom	1969
2.	Bernice Rubens	*The Elected Member*	United Kingdom	1970
3.	V. S. Naipaul	*In a Free State* (short story)	United Kingdom / Trinidad & Tobago	1971
4.	John Berger	G.	United Kingdom	1972
5.	J. G. Farrell	*The Siege of Krishnapur*	United Kingdom/ Ireland	1973
6.	Stanley Middleton	*Holiday*	United Kingdom	1974
7.	Nadine Gordimer	*The Conservationist*	South Africa	1974
8.	Ruth Prawer Jhabvala	*Heat and Dust*	United Kingdom/ Germany	1975

Sl.no	Winner	Novel	Country	Year
9.	David Storey	*Saville*	United Kingdom	1976
10.	Paul Scott	*Staying On,*	United Kingdom	1977
11.	Iris Murdoch	*The Sea, The Sea*	Ireland/ United Kingdom	1978
12.	Penelope Fitzgerald	*Offshore*	United Kingdom	1979
13.	William Golding	*Rites of Passage*	United Kingdom	1980
14.	Salman Rushdie	*Midnight's Children*	United Kingdom/ India	1981
15.	Thomas Keneally	*Schindler's Ark*	Australia	1982
16.	J. M. Coetzee	*Life & Times of Michael K*	South Africa	1983
17.	Anita Brookner	*Hotel du Lac*	United Kingdom	1984
18.	Keri Hulme	*The Bone People*	New Zealand	1985

Sl.no	Winner	Novel	Country	Year
19.	Kingsley Amis	*The Old Devils*	United Kingdom	1986
20.	Penelope Lively	*Moon Tiger*	United Kingdom	1987
21.	Kazuo Ishiguro	*Oscar and Lucinda*	Australia	1988
22.	Peter Carey	*The Remains of the Day*	United Kingdom/ Japan	1989
23.	A. S. Byatt	*Possession*	United Kingdom	1990
24.	Ben Okri	*The Famished Road*	Nigeria	1991
25.	Michael Ondaatje	*The English Patient*	Canada / Sri Lanka	1992
26.	Barry Unsworth	*Sacred Hunger*	United Kingdom	1992
27.	Roddy Doyle	*Paddy Clarke Ha Ha Ha*	Ireland	1993

Sl.no	Winner	Novel	Country	Year
28.	James Kelman	*How Late It Was, How Late*	United Kingdom	1994
29.	Pat Barker	*The Ghost Road*	United Kingdom	1995
30.	Graham Swift	*Last Orders*	United Kingdom	1996
31.	Arundhati Roy	*The God of Small Things*	India	1997
32.	Ian McEwan	*Amsterdam*	United Kingdom	1998
33.	J. M. Coetzee	*Disgrace*	South Africa	1999
34.	Margaret Atwood	*The Blind Assassin*	Canada	2000
35.	Peter Carey	*True History of the Kelly Gang*	Australia	2001
36.	Yann Martel	*Life of Pi*	Canada	2002
37.	DBC Pierre	*Vernon God Little*	Australia	2003
38.	Alan Hollinghurst	*The Line of Beauty*	United Kingdom	2004

Sl.no	Winner	Novel	Country	Year
39.	John Banville	*The Sea*	Ireland	2005
40.	Kiran Desai	*The Inheritance of Loss*	India	2006
41.	Anne Enright	*The Gathering*	Ireland	2007
42.	Aravind Adiga	*The White Tiger*	India	2008
43.	Hilary Mantel	*Wolf Hall*	United Kingdom	2009
44.	Howard Jacobson	*The Finkler Question*	United Kingdom	2010
45.	Julian Barnes	*The Sense of an Ending*	United Kingdom	2011
46.	Hilary Mantel	*Bring Up The Bodies*	United Kingdom	2012
47.	Eleanor Catton	*The Luminaries*	Canada/ New Zealand	2013

Sl.no	Winner	Novel	Country	Year
48.	Richard Flanagan	*The Narrow Road to the Deep North*	Australia	2014
49.	Marlon James	*A Brief History of Seven Killings*	Jamaica	2015
50.	Paul Beatty	*The Sellout*	United States	2016
51.	George Saunders	*Lincoln in the Bardo*	United States	2017
52.	Anna Burns	*Milkman*	United Kingdom/ Northern Ireland	2018
53.	Bernardine Evaristo	*Girl, Woman, Other*	United Kingdom	2019
54.	Margaret Atwood	*The Testaments*	Canada	2019
55.	Douglas Stuart	*Shuggie Bain*	United Kingdom / United States	2020

Sl.no	Winner	Novel	Country	Year
56.	Damon Galgut	*The Promise*	South Africa	2021
57.	Shehan Karunatilaka	*The Seven Moons of Maali Almeida*	Sri Lanka	2022

List of Pulitzer Prize For Novel & Fiction Winners and Their Work

The Pulitzer Prizes were instituted by Joseph Pulitzer in 1917, were given not only to journalistic genres but also literary and non-literary genres viz., poetry, fiction and drama, etc., annually. In his original plan of awards, there was also a prize for merits in the field of literature and they are revered as one of the greatest accolades recognised in American publishing industry and serve as an excellence in a particular genre.

The Pulitzer for Fiction was first given in 1918 and until 1948, the Prize was essentially given to novels and later changed as Fiction and the eligibility criteria was expanded to include short stories, novellas, novelettes and novels. It is interesting to note that the award was primarily thought for encouragement of writers outside for the journalistic areas.

The original definition was "… for the American novel published during the year which shall best present the wholsesome atmosphere of American life, and the highest standard of American manners and manhood" (Fischer and Fischer *Fiction* 3). Then, it was changed as "for the American novel published during the year, preferably one which shall best present the whole atmosphere of American life" (Fischer and Fischer *Fiction* 8). However, its present definition is "distinguished fiction in book form during the year by an American author, preferably dealing with American life" (Fischer and Fischer *Fiction* 8).

Sl. no	Winner(s)	Work(s)	Remarks (if any)	Year
1.	Ernest Poole	*His Family*		1918
2.	Booth Tarkington	*The Magnificent Ambersons*		1919
3.	Edith Wharton	*The Age of Innocence*		1921
4.	Booth Tarkington	*Alice Adams*		1922
5.	Willa Cather	*One of Ours*		1923
6.	Margaret Wilson	*The Able McLaughlins*		1924
7.	Edna Ferber	*So Big*		1925
8.	Sinclair Lewis	*Arrowsmith*		1926
9.	Louis Bromfield	*Early Autumn*		1927

Sl. no	Winner(s)	Work(s)	Remarks (if any)	Year
10.	Thornton Wilder	*The Bride of San Luis Rey*		1928
11.	Julia Peterkin	*Scarlet Sister*		1929
12.	Oliver Lafarge	*Laughing Boy*		1930
13.	Margaret Ayer Barnes	*Years of Grace*		1931
14.	Pearl S. Buck	*The Good Earth*		1932
15.	T.S. Stribling	*The Store*		1933
16.	Caroline Miller	*Lamb in His Bosom*		1934
17.	Josephine Winslow Johnson	*Now in November*		1935
18.	Harold L. Davis	*Honey in the Horn*		1936
19.	Maragaret Mitchell	*Gone with the Wind*		1937
20.	John Phillips	*The Late George Apley*		1938

Sl. no	Winner(s)	Work(s)	Remarks (if any)	Year
21.	Marjorie Kinnan	*The Yearling*		1939
22.	John Steinbeck	*The Grapes of Wrath*		1940
23.	Ellen Glasgow	*In This Our Life*		1942
24.	Upton Sinclair	*Dragon's Teeth*		1943
25.	Martin Flavin	*Journey in the Dark*		1944
26.	John Hersey	*A Bell for Adams*		1945
27.	Robert Penn Warren	*All the King's Men*		1947
28.	James A. Mitchener	*Tales of the South Pacific*		1948
29.	James Gould	*Guard of Honor*		1949
30.	A.B. Guthrie	*The Way West*		1950
31.	Conrad Ritcher	*The Town*		1951

Sl. no	Winner(s)	Work(s)	Remarks (if any)	Year
32.	Herman Wouk	*The Caine Mutiny*		1952
33.	Ernest Hemingway	*The Old Man and the Sea*		1953
34.	William Faulkner	*A Fable*		1955
35.	MacKinlay Kantor	*Andersonville*		1956
36.	James Agree	*A Death In the Family*		1958
37.	Robert Lewis Taylor	*The Travels of Jaimie McPheeters*		1959
38.	Allen Drury	*Advise and Consent*		1960
39.	Harper Lee	*To Kill a Mockingbird*		1961
40.	Edwin O' Connor	*The Edge of Sadness*		1962
41.	William Faulkner	*The Reivers*		1963

Sl. no	Winner(s)	Work(s)	Remarks (if any)	Year
42.		NO AWARD		1964
43.	Shirley Ann Grau	*The Keepers of the House*		1965
44.	Katherine Anne Porter	*Collected Stories*		1966
45.	Bernard Malamud	*The Fixer*		1967
46.	William Styron	*The Confessions of Nat Turner*		1968
47.	N. Scott Momaday	*House Made of Dawn*		1969
48.	Jean Stafford	*Collected Stories*		1970
49.	Wallace Stegner	*Angle of Repose*		1972
50.	Eudora Welty	*The Optimist's Daughter*		1973
51.	Michael Shaara	*The Killer Angels*		1975
52.	Saul Bellow	*Humbolt's Gift*		1976

Sl. no	Winner(s)	Work(s)	Remarks (if any)	Year
53.	James Alan McPherson	*Elbow's Room*		1978
54.	John Cheever	*The Stories of John Cheever*		1979
55.	Norman Mailer	*The Executioner's Song*		1980
56.	John Kennedy Toole	*A Confederacy of Dunces*		1981
57.	John Updike	*Rabbit is Rich*		1982
58.	Alice Walker	*The Color Purple*		1983
59.	William Kennedy	*Ironweed*		1984
60.	Alison Lurie	*Foreign Affairs*		1985
61.	Larry McMurtry	*Lonesome Dove*		1986
62.	Peter Taylor	*A Summons to Memphis*		1987

Sl. no	Winner(s)	Work(s)	Remarks (if any)	Year
63.	Toni Morrison	*Beloved*		1988
64.	Anne Taylor	*Breathing Lessons*		1989
65.	Oscar Hijuelos	*The Mambo Kings Play Songs of Love*		1990
66.	John Updike	*Rabbit at Rest*		1991
67.	Jane Smiley	*A Thousand Acres*		1992
68.	Robert Olen Butler	*A Good Scent from a Strange Mountain*		1993
69.	E. Annie Proulx	*The Shipping News*		1994
70.	Carol Shields	*The Stone Diaries*		1995
71.	Richard Ford	*nIndependence Day*		1996

Sl. no	Winner(s)	Work(s)	Remarks (if any)	Year
72	Martin Dressler	*The Tale of an American Dreamer*		1997
73.	Philip Roth	*American Pastoral*		1998
74.	Micheal Cunningham	*The Hours*		1999
75.	Jhumpa Lahiri	*Interpreter of Maladies*		2000
76.	Michael Chabon	*The Amazing Adventures of Kavalier & Clay*		2001
77.	Richard Ross	*Empire Falls*		2002
78.	Jeffrey Eugenides	*Middlesex*		2003
79.	Edward P. Jones	*The Known World*		2004
80.	Marilynne Robinson	*Gilead*		2005

Sl. no	Winner(s)	Work(s)	Remarks (if any)	Year
81.	Geraldine Brooks	*March*		2006
82.	Cormac McCarthy	*The Road*		2007
83.	Junot Diaz	*The Brief Wondrous Life of Oscar Wao*		2008
84.	Elizabeth Strout	*Olive Kitteridge*	A Collection of 13 short stories set in small-town Maine that packs a cumulative emotional wallop, bound together by polished prose and by Olive, the title character, blunt, flawed and fascinating.	2009

Sl. no	Winner(s)	Work(s)	Remarks (if any)	Year
85.	Paul Harding	*Tinkers*	A powerful celebration of life in which a New England father and son, through suffering and joy, transcend their imprisoning lives and offer new ways of perceiving the world and mortality	2010

Sl. no	Winner(s)	Work(s)	Remarks (if any)	Year
86.	Jennifer Egan	*A Visit from the Goon Squad*	An inventive investigative of growing up and growing old in the digital age, displaying a big-hearted curiosity about cultural change at warp speed.	2011

Sl. no	Winner(s)	Work(s)	Remarks (if any)	Year
87.		NO AWARD		2012
88.	Adam Johnson	*The Orphan Master's Son*	An exquisitely crafted novel that carries the reader on an adventuresome journey into the depths of totalitarian North Korea and into the most intimate spaces of the human heart	2013

Sl. no	Winner(s)	Work(s)	Remarks (if any)	Year
89.	Donna Tartt	*The Goldfinch*	A beautifully written coming-of-age novel with exquisitely drawn characters that follows a grieving boy's entanglements with a small famous painting that has eluded destruction, a book that stimulates the mind and touches the heart	2014

Sl. no	Winner(s)	Work(s)	Remarks (if any)	Year
90.	Anthony Doerr	*All the Light We Cannot See*	An imaginative and inspired by the horror of World War II and written in short, elegant chapters that explore human nature and the contradictory power of technology	2015

Sl. no	Winner(s)	Work(s)	Remarks (if any)	Year
91.	Viet Thanh Nguyen	*The Sympathizer*	A layered immigrant tale told in the wry, confessional voice of a "man of two minds" - and two countries Vietnam and United States	2016
92.	Colson Whitehead	*The Underground Railroad*	For a smart melding of realism and allegory that combines the violence of salvery and the drama of escape in a myth that speaks of contemporary America	2017

Sl. no	Winner(s)	Work(s)	Remarks (if any)	Year
93.	Andrew Sean Greer	*Less*	A generous book, musical in its prose and expansive in its structure and range, about growing older and the essential nature of loss	2018
94.	Richard Powers	*The Overstory*	An ingeniously structured narrative that branches and canopies like the trees at the core of the story whose wonder and connectivity echo those of the human living amongst them	2019

Sl. no	Winner(s)	Work(s)	Remarks (if any)	Year
95.	Colson Whitehead	*The Nickel Boys*	A space and devastating exploration of abuse at a reform school in Jim Crow-era Florid that is ultimately a powerful tale of human perseverance, dignity and redemption	2020

Sl. no	Winner(s)	Work(s)	Remarks (if any)	Year
96.	Louise Erdrich	*The Night Watchman*	A majestic, polyphonic novel about a community's efforts to halt the proposed displacement and elimination of several Native American tribes in the 1950s, rendered with dexterity and imagination	2021

Sl. no	Winner(s)	Work(s)	Remarks (if any)	Year
97.	Joshua Cohen	*The Netanyahus: An Account of a Minor and Ultimately Even Negligible Episode in the History of a Very Famous Family*	A mordant, linguistically deft historical novel about the ambiguities of the Jewish-American experience, presenting ideas and disputes as volatile as its tightly-wound plot.	2022

Sl. no	Winner(s)	Work(s)	Remarks (if any)	Year
98.	Barbara Kingsolver	*Demon Copperhead*	A masterful recasting of "David Copperfield" narrated by an Appalachian boy whose wise, unwavering voice related his encounters with poverty, addiction, intuitional failures and moral collapse – and his efforts to conquer them	2023

Sl. no	Winner(s)	Work(s)	Remarks (if any)	Year
99.	Hernan Diaz	*Trust*	A riveting novel set in a bygone America that explores family, wealth and ambition through linked narratives rendered in different literary styles, a complex examination of love and power in a country where capitalism is king.	2023

List of Pulitzer Prize For Drama Winners and Their Work

The original definition for Pulitzer Prize for Drama stated during the inception of the Prize, in 1917, was thus: "the original American play, performed in New York, which shall represent the educational value and the power of the stage in raising the standard of good morals, good taste, and good manners". However, by 1929, the clause "raising the standard …" was omitted and the present form, "For a distinguished play by an American author, preferably original in its source and dealing with American life" (qtd. in Adler, Mirror xi).

Sl. no	Winner(s)	Work(s)	Remarks (if any)	Year
1.	Jesse Lynch Williams	*Why Marry?*		1918
2.	Eugene O'Neill	*Beyond the Horizon*		1920
3.	Zona Gale	*Miss Lulu Bett*		1921
4.	Eugene O'Neill	*Anna Christie*		1922
5.	Owen Davis	*Icebound*		1923
6.	Hatcher Hughes	*Hell-Bent Fer Heaven*		1924
7.	Sidney Howard	*They Knew What They Wanted*		1925
8.	George Kelly	*Craig's Wife*		1926

Sl. no	Winner(s)	Work(s)	Remarks (if any)	Year
9.	Paul Green	*In Abraham's Bosom*		1927
10.	Eugene O'Neill	*Strange Interlude*		1928
11.	Elmer L. Rice	*Street Scene*		1929
12.	Marc Connelly	*The Green Pastures*		1930
13.	Susan Glaspell	*Alison's House*		1931
14.	George S. Kaufman, Morrie Ryskind and Ira Gershwin	*Of Thee I Sing*		1932
15.	Maxwell Anderson	*Both Your Houses*		1933

Sl. no	Winner(s)	Work(s)	Remarks (if any)	Year
16.	Sidney Kingsley	*Men in White*		1934
17.	Zoe Akins	*The Old Maid*		1935
18.	Robert E. Sherwood	*Idiots Delight*		1936
19.	Moss Hart and George S. Kaufman	*You Can't Take It With You*		1937
20.	Thornton Wilder	*Our Town*		1938
21.	Robert E. Sherwood	*Abe Lincoln in Illinois*		1939

Sl. no	Winner(s)	Work(s)	Remarks (if any)	Year
22.	William Saroyan	*The Time of Your Life*		1940
23.	Robert E. Sherwood	*There Shall Be No Night*		1941
24.	Thornton Wilder	*The Skin of Our Teeth*		1943
25.	Mary Chase	*Harvey*		1945
26.	Russel Crouse and Howard Lindsay	*State of the Union*		1946
27.	Tennessee Williams	*A Streetcar Named Desire*		1948

Sl. no	Winner(s)	Work(s)	Remarks (if any)	Year
28.	Arthur Miller	*Death of a Salesman*		1949
29.	Richard Rodgers, Oscar Hammerstein II and Joshua Logan	*South Pacific*		1950
30.	Joseph Kramm	*The Strike*		1952
31.	William Inge	*Picnic*		1953
32.	John Patrick	*The Teahouse of the August Moon*		1954
33.	Tennessee Williams	*Cat on a Hot Tin Roof*		1955

Sl. no	Winner(s)	Work(s)	Remarks (if any)	Year
34.	Albert Hackett and Frances Goodrich	*Diary of Anne Frank*		1956
35.	Eugene O'Neill	*Long Day's Journey Into Night*		1957
36.	Ketti Frings	*Look Homeward, Angel*		1958
37.	Archibald Macleish	*J.B.,*		1959

Sl. no	Winner(s)	Work(s)	Remarks (if any)	Year
38.	Jerome Weidman, George Abbott, Jerry Bock, Sheldon Harnick	*Firello!*		1960
39.	Tad Mosel	*All the Way Home*		1961
40.	Frank Losser and Abe Burrows	*How to Succeed In Business Without Really Trying*		1962
41.	Frank D. Gilory	*The Subject Was Roses*		1965
42.	Edward Albee	*A Delicate Balance*		1967

Sl. no	Winner(s)	Work(s)	Remarks (if any)	Year
43.	Howard Sackler	*The Great White Hope*		1969
44.	Charles Gordone	*No Place To Be Somebody*		1970
45.	Paul Zindel	*The Effect of Gamma Rays on Man-In-The-Moon Marigolds*		1971
46.	Jason Miller	*That Championship Season*		1973
47.	Edward Albee	*Seascape*		1975

Sl. no	Winner(s)	Work(s)	Remarks (if any)	Year
48.	Michael Bennett, James Kirkwood, Jr., Marvin Hamlisch, Nicholas Dante and Edward Kleban	*A Chorus Line*		1976
49.	Michael Cristofer	*The Shadow Box*		1977
50.	Donald L. Coburn	*The Gin Game*		1978
51.	Sam Shepard	*Buried Child*		1979

Sl. no	Winner(s)	Work(s)	Remarks (if any)	Year
52.	Langford Wilson	*Talley's Folly*		1980
53.	Beth Henley	*Crimes of the Heart*		1981
54.	Charles Fuller	*A Soldier's Play*		1982
55.	Marsha Norman	*'Night, Mother*		1983
56.	David Mamet	*Glengarry Glen Ross*		1984
57.	Stephen Sondheim and James Lapine	*Sunday in the Park With George*		1985
58.	August Wilson	*Fences*		1987

Sl. no	Winner(s)	Work(s)	Remarks (if any)	Year
59.	Alfred Uhry	*Driving Miss Daisy*		1988
60.	Wendy Wasserstein	*The Heidi Chronicles*		1989
61.	August Wilson	*The Piano Lesson*		1990
62.	Neil Simon	*Lost in Yonkers*		1991
63.	Robert Schenkkan	*The Kentucky Cycle*		1992
64.	Tony Kushner	*Angels in American: Millennium Approaches*		1993
65.	Edward Albee	*Three Tall Women*		1994

Sl. no	Winner(s)	Work(s)	Remarks (if any)	Year
66.	Horton Foote	*The Young Man From Atlanta*		1995
67.	Jonathan Larson	*Rent*		1996
68.			NO AWARD	1997
69.	Paula Vogel	*How I Learned to Drive*		1998
70.	Margaret Edson	*Wit*		1999
71.	Donald Margulies	*Dinner with Friends*		2000
72	David Auburn	*Proof*		2001

Sl. no	Winner(s)	Work(s)	Remarks (if any)	Year
73.	Suzan-Lori Parks	*Topdog/Underdog*		2002
74.	Nilo Cruz	*Anna in the Tropics*		2003
75.	Doug Wright	*I am My Own Wife*		2004
76.	John Patrick Shanley	*Doubt, a Parable*		2005
77.		NO AWARD		2006
78.	David Lindsay-Abaire	Rabbit Hole		2007
79.	Tracy Letts	*August: Osage County*		2008

Sl. no	Winner(s)	Work(s)	Remarks (if any)	Year
80.	Lynn Nottage	*Ruined*	A scaring drama set in chaotic Congo that compels audience to face the horror of wartime rape and brutality while still finding affirmation of life and hope amid hopelessness	2009
81.	Tom Kitt and Brian Yorkey	*Next to Normal*	A powerful rock musical that grapples with mental illness in a suburban family and expands the scope of subject matter for musicals	2010
82.	Bruce Norris	*Clybourne Park*	A Powerful work whose memorable characters speak in witty and perceptive ways to America's sometimes toxic struggle with race and class consciousness	2011

Sl. no	Winner(s)	Work(s)	Remarks (if any)	Year
83.	Quiara Alegria Hudes	*Water by the Spoonful*	An Imaginative Play about the search for meaning by a returning Iraq war veteran while working in a sandwich shop in his hometown of Philadelphia	2012
84.	Ayad Akhtar	*Disgraced*	A moving play that depicts a successful corporate lawyer painfully forced to consider why he has for so long camouflage his Pakistani Muslim heritage	2013
85.	Annie Baker	*The Flick*	A thoughtful drama with well-crafted characters that focuses on three employees of a Massachusetts art-house movie theatre. Rendering lives rarely seen on the stage	2014

Sl. no	Winner(s)	Work(s)	Remarks (if any)	Year
86.	Stephen Adly Guirgis	*Between Riverside and Crazy*	A nuanced, beautifully written play about a retired police officer faced with eviction that uses dark comedy to confront questions of life and death	2015
87.	Lin-Manuel Miranda	*Hamilton*	A landmark American musical about the gifted and self-destructive founding father whose story becomes both contemporary and irresistable	2016
88.	Lynn Nottage	*Sweat*	For a nuanced yet powerful drama that reminds audiences of the stacked deck still facing workers searching for the American dream	2017

Sl. no	Winner(s)	Work(s)	Remarks (if any)	Year
89.	Martyna Majok	*Cost of Living*	An honest, original work that invites audiences to examine diverse perceptions of privilege and human connection through two pairs of mismatched individuals: a former trucker and his recently paralyzed ex-wife, and an arrogant young man with cerebral palsy and his new caregiver	2018
90.	Jackie Sibblies Drury	*Fairview*	A hard-hitting drama that examines race in a highly conceptual, layered structure, ultimately bringing audience into the actors' community to deep-seated prejudices	2019

Sl. no	Winner(s)	Work(s)	Remarks (if any)	Year
91.	Michael R. Jackson	*A Strange Loop*	A metafictional musical that tracks the creative process of an artist transforming issues of identity, race and sexuality that once pushed him to margins of the cultural mainstream into a meditation on universal human fears and insecurities	2020
92.	Katori Hall	*The Hot Wing King*	A Funny, deeply felt consideration of Black masculinity and how it is perceived, filtered through the experiences of a loving gay couple and their extended family as they prepare for a culinary competition.	2021

Sl. no	Winner(s)	Work(s)	Remarks (if any)	Year
93.	James Ijames	*Fat Ham*	A funny, poignant play that deftly transposes "Hamlet" to a family barbecue in the American South to grapple with questions of identity, kinship, responsibility, and honesty.	2022
94.	Sanaz Toosi	*English*	A quietly powerful play about four Iranian adults preparing for an English language exam in a storefront school near Tehran, where family separations and travel restrictions drive them to learn a new language that may alter their identities and also represent a new life.	2023

List of Pulitzer Prize For Poetry Winners and Their Work(S)

According to John Hohenberg, Joseph Pulitzer had a "little interest in American poetry" and "he had omitted any mention of poetry from his will" (Fischer and Fischer *Poetry* 3). In consequence, there was "no poetry prize in the original plan of Awards" (Fischer and Fischer *Poetry* 3). When the first Pulitzer Prize were awarded in 1917 and a category for poetry or verse was lacking, this was discovered by a member of the newly established Poetry Society of America. At the same time, when the interests of the poetry society and Columbia coincided, it led to a poetry Prize which was awarded in 1918 and is regarded as the forerunner of the later Pulitzer Prize for Poetry. Though it was first presented in 1922, it was earlier called as the Columbia University Poetry Prize.

Sl. no	Winner(s)	Work(s)	Remarks (if any)	Year
1.	Sara Teasdale	Love Songs	A special grant from The Poetry Society	1918
2.	Carl Sandburg	*Corn Huskers*	A special grant from The Poetry Society	1919
3.	Margaret Widdemer	The Old Road to Paradise	A special grant from The Poetry Society	1919
4.	Edwin Arlington Robinson	Collected Poems		1922

Sl. no	Winner(s)	Work(s)	Remarks (if any)	Year
5.	Edna St. Vincent Millay	*The Ballad of the Harp-Weaver, A Few Figs from Thistles, Eight Sonnets in 'American Poetry' 1922: A Miscellany*		1923
6.	Robert Frost	*New Hampshire*		1924
7.	Edwin Arlington Robinson	The Man Who Died Twice		1925
8.	Amy Lowell	*What's O'Clock*		1926

Sl. no	Winner(s)	Work(s)	Remarks (if any)	Year
9.	Leonora Speyer	*Fiddler's Farewell*		1927
10.	Edwin Arlington Robinson	*Tristram*		1928
11.	Stephen Vincent Benet	John Brown's Body		1929
12.	Conrad Aiken	*Selected Poems*		1930
13.	Robert Frost	*Collected Poems*		1931
14.	George Hill Dilon	*The Flowering Stone*		1932

Sl. no	Winner(s)	Work(s)	Remarks (if any)	Year
15.	Archibald MacLeish	Conquistador		1933
16.	Robert Hillyer	*Collected Verse*		1934
17.	Audrey Wurdermann	*Bright Ambush*		1935
18.	Robert P.T. Coffin	*Strange Holiness*		1936
19.	Robert Frost	A Further Range		1937
20.	Marya Zaturenska	*Cold Morning Sky*		1938
21.	John Gould Fletcher	*Selected Poems*		1939

Sl. no	Winner(s)	Work(s)	Remarks (if any)	Year
22.	Mark Van Doren	*Collected Poems*		1940
23.	Leonard Bacon	Sunderland Capture		1941
24.	William Rose Benet	*The Dust Which is God*		1942
25.	Robert Frost	*A Witness Tree*		1943
26.	Stephen Vincent Benet	*Western Star*		1944
27.	Karl Shapiro	V-Letter and Other Poems		1945

Sl. no	Winner(s)	Work(s)	Remarks (if any)	Year
28.			No Award Given	1946
29.	Robert Lowell	*Lord Weary's Castle*		1947
30.	W.H. Auden	*The Age of Anxiety*		1948
31.	Peter Viereck	*Terror and Decorum*		1949
32.	Gwendolyn Brooks	*Annie Allen*		1950
33.	Carl sandburg	*complete poems*		1951
34.	Marianne Moore	*Collected poems*		1952

Sl. no	Winner(s)	Work(s)	Remarks (if any)	Year
35.	Archibald Macleish	*Collected Poems 1917- 1952*		1953
36.	Theodore Roethke	*the walking*		1954
37.	Wallace Stevens	*Collected Poems*		1955
38.	Elizabeth Bishop	*Poems: North and South*		1956
39.	Richard Wilbur	Things of This World		1957
40.	Robert Penn Warren	Promises: Poems, 1954-1956		1958

Sl. no	Winner(s)	Work(s)	Remarks (if any)	Year
41.	Stanley Kunitz	Selected Poems 1928 - 1958		1959
42.	W.D. Snodgrass	Heart's Needle		1960
43.	Phyllis McGinley	Times Three: Selected Verse from Three Decades		1961
44.	Alan Dugan	Poems		1962
45.	William Carolos Williams	Pictures from Brueghel		1963

Sl. no	Winner(s)	Work(s)	Remarks (if any)	Year
46.	Louis Simpson	At the End of the Open Road		1964
47.	John Berryman	77 Dream Songs		1965
48.	Richard Eberhart	Selected Poems		1966
49.	Anne Sexton	Live or Die		1967
50.	Anthony Hecht	The Hard Hours		1968
51.	George Oppen	Of Being Numerous		1969

Sl. no	Winner(s)	Work(s)	Remarks (if any)	Year
52.	Richard Howard	*United Subjects*		1970
53.	William S. Merwin	*The Carrier of Ladders*		1971
54.	James Wright	*Collected Poems*		1972
55.	Maxine Kumin	Up Country		1973
56.	Robert Lowell	*The Dolphin*		1974
57.	Gary Snyder	*Turtle Island*		1975
58.	John Ashbery	*Self-Portrait in a Convex Mirror*		1976

Sl. no	Winner(s)	Work(s)	Remarks (if any)	Year
59.	James Merill	Divine Comedies		1977
60.	Howard Nemerov	*Collected Poems*		1978
61.	Robert Penn Warren	*Now and Then*		1979
62.	Donald Justice	*Selected Poems*		1980
63.	James Schuyler	The Morning of the Poem		1981
64.	Sylvia Plath	*The Collected Poems*		1982
65.	Galway Kinnell	*Selected Poems*		1983

Sl. no	Winner(s)	Work(s)	Remarks (if any)	Year
66.	Mary Oliver	*American Primitive*		1984
67.	Carolyn Kizer	Yin		1985
68.	Henry S. Taylor	*The Flying Change*		1986
69.	Rita Dove	*Thomas and Beulah*		1987
70.	William Merdith	*Partial Accounts: New and Selected Poems*		1988
71.	Richard Wilbur	New and Collected Poems		1989

Sl. no	Winner(s)	Work(s)	Remarks (if any)	Year
72.	Charles Simic	*The World Doesn't End*		1990
73.	Mna Van Duyn	*Near Changes*		1991
74.	James Tate	*Selected Poems*		1992
75.	Louise Gluck	The Wild Iris		1993
76.	Yusuf Komunyakaa	*Neon Vernacular: New and Selected Poems*		1994
77.	Philip Levine	*The Simple Truth*		1995
78.	Jorie Graham	*The Dream of the Unified Field*		1996

Sl. no	Winner(s)	Work(s)	Remarks (if any)	Year
79.	Lisel Mueller	Alive Together: New and Selected Poems		1997
80.	Charles Wright	Black Zodiac		1998
81.	Mark Strand	Blizzard of One		1999
82.	C.K. Williams	Repair		2000
83.	Stephen Dunn	Different Hours		2001
84.	Carl Dennis	Practical Gods		2002
85.	Paul Muldoon	Moy Sand and Gravel		2003

Sl. no	Winner(s)	Work(s)	Remarks (if any)	Year
86.	Franz Wright	*Walking to Martha's Vineyard*		2004
87.	Ted Kooser	Delights & Shadows		2005
88.	Claudia Emerson	*Late Wife*		2006
89	Natasha Tretheway	*Native Guard*		2007
90.	Robert Hass	*Times and Materials*		2008
91.	Philip Schultz	Failure		2008

Sl. no	Winner(s)	Work(s)	Remarks (if any)	Year
92..	W.S. Merwin	*The Shadow of Sirius*	A Collection of luminous, often tender poems that focus on the profound power of memory	2009
93..	Rae Armantrout	*Versed*	A book striking for its wit and linguistic inventiveness, offering poems that are often little thought-bombs detonating in the mind long after the first reading	2010
94..	Kay Ryan	*The Best of It: New and Selected Poems*	A body of work spanning 45 years, witty, rebellious and yet tender, a treasure trove of an iconoclast and joyful mind	2011
95..	Tracy K. Smith	*Life of Mars*	A collection of bold skill poems, taking readers into the universe and moving them to an authentic mix of joy and pain	2012

Sl. no	Winner(s)	Work(s)	Remarks (if any)	Year
96.	Sharon Olds	*Stag's Leap*	A book of unflinching poems on the author's dicorce that examine love, sorrow and the limits of self-knowledge	2013
97.	Vijay Seshadri	*3 Selections*	A compelling collection of poems that examine human consciousness, from birth to dementia, in a voice that is by turns witty and grave, compassionate and remorseless	2014
98.	Gregory Pardlo	*Digest*	Clear-voiced poems that bring readers the news from 21st century America, rich with thought, ideas and histories public and private	2015

Sl. no	Winner(s)	Work(s)	Remarks (if any)	Year
99.	Peter Balakian	*Ozone Journal*	Poems that bear witness to the old losses and tragedies that undergird a global age of danger and uncertainty	2016
100.	Tyehimba Jess	*Olio*	For a distinctive work that mends performance art with the deeper art of poetry to explore collective memory and challenge contemporary notions of race and identity	2017
101.	Frank Bidart	*Half-light: Collected Poems 1965-2016*	A Volume of unyielding ambition and remarkable scope that mixes long dramatic poems with short elliptical lyrics, building on classical mythology and reinventing forms of desires that defy societal norms.	2018

Sl. no	Winner(s)	Work(s)	Remarks (if any)	Year
102.	Forrest Gander	*Be With*	A Collection of elegies that grapple with sudden loss and the difficulties of expressing grief and yearning for the departed	2019
103.	Jericho Brown	*The Tradition*	A Collection of masterful lyrics that combine delicacy with historical urgency in their loving evocation of bodies vulnerable to hostility and violence	2020
104.	Natalie Diaz	*Postcolonial Love Poem*	A collection of tender, heart-wrenching and defiant poems that explodes what it means to love and be loved in an America beset by conflict	2021

Sl. no	Winner(s)	Work(s)	Remarks (if any)	Year
105.	Diana Seuss	*Frank: Sonnets*	A virtuosic collection that inventively expands the sonnet form to confront the messy contradictions of contemporary America, including the beauty and the difficulty of working-class life in the Rust Belt.	2022
106.	Carl Phillips	*Then the War: And Selected Poems, 2007 – 2020*	A masterful collection that chronicles American culture as the country struggles to make sense of its politics, of life in the wake of a pandemic, and of our place in a changing global community.	2023

List of American Poet Laureates

Unlike the British Counterpart, the American poet Laureate acts as a chair of poetry for the Library of Congress. He is not a salaried member but is expected to present one major poetic work and appear at certain national ceremonies. According to the Library of Congress website, "as the nation's official poet, the Poet Laureate consultant in Poetry in the Library of Congress seeks to raise the national consciousness to a greater appreciation of the reading and writing of poetry" (web).

Sl.no	Poet(s)	Period of Laureateship
1.	Joseph Auslander	1937-1941
2.	Allen Tate	1943-1944
3.	Robert Penn Warren	1944-1945
4.	Louise Bogan	1945-1946
5.	Karl Shapiro	1946-1947
6.	Robert Lowell	1947-1948

Sl.no	Poet(s)	Period of Laureateship
7.	Leonie Adams	1948-1949
8.	Elizabeth Bishop	1949-1950
9.	Conrad Aiken (first to serve twice)	1950-1952
10.	William Carlos Williams	(appointed in 1952 but did not serve)
11.	Randall Jarrell	1956-1958
12.	Robert Frost	1958-1959
13.	Richard Eberhart	1959-1961
14.	Louis Untermeyer	1961-1963
15.	Howard Nemerov	1963-1964
16.	Reed Whittemore	1964-1965
17.	Stephen Spender	1965-1966
18.	James Dickey	1966-1968
19.	William Jay Smith	1968-1970
20.	William Stafford	1970-1971
21.	Josephine Jacobsen	1971-1973
22.	Daniel Hoffman	1973-1974

Sl.no	Poet(s)	Period of Laureateship
23.	Stanley Kunitz	1974-1976
24.	Robert Hayden	1976-1978
25.	William Meredith	1978-1980
26.	Maxine Kumin	1981-1982
27.	Anthony Hecht	1982-1984
28.	Robert Fitzgerald	1984-1985
29.	Reed Whittemore	1984-1985 (interim Consultant in Poetry)
30.	Gwendolyn Brooks	1985-1986
31.	Robert Penn Warren	1986-1987 (first to be designated Poet Laureate Consultant in Poetry)
32.	Richard Wilbur	1987-1988
33.	Howard Nemerov	1988-1990
34.	Mark Strand	1990-1991
35.	Joseph Brodsky	1991-1992
36.	Mona Van Duyn	1992-1993
37.	Rita Dove	1993-1995

Sl.no	Poet(s)	Period of Laureateship
38.	Robert Hass	1995-1997
39.	Robert Pinsky	1997-2000
40.	Stanley Kunitz	2000-2001
41.	Billy Collins	2001-2003
42.	Louise Gluck	2003-2004
43.	Ted Kooser	2004-2006
44.	Donald Hall	2006-2007
45.	Charles Simic	2007-2008
46.	Kay Ryan	2008-2010
47.	W.S. Merwin	2010-2011
48.	Philip Levine	2011-2012
49.	Natasha Trethewey	2012-2014
50.	Charles Wright	2014-2015
51.	Juan Felipe Herrera	2015-2017
52.	Tracy K. Smith	2017-2019
53.	Joy Harjo	2019 – 2022
54.	Ada Limón	2022 onwards

List of British Poet Laureates

The title "poet laureate" [emphasis mine] was first given in England in the 17th century for outstanding poetry. Although the position's incumbent is a paid employee of the British royal household, it no longer carries any specific lyrical responsibilities. A comparable position was established in the US in 1936.

The British Poet Laureate is an honorary position chosen by the British monarch, who currently acts on the prime minister's advice. The post does not require any specific obligations, however there is an expectation that the holder will produce verse for key national occasions.

Sl.no	Poet(s)	Period of Laureateship
1.	John Dryden	1670-1689
2.	Thomas Shadwell	1689-1692
3.	Nahum Tate	1692-1715
4.	Nicholas Rowe	1715-1718
5.	Laurence Eusden	1718-1730

Sl.no	Poet(s)	Period of Laureateship
6.	Colley Cibber	1730-1757
7.	William Whitehead	1757-1785
8.	Thomas Warton	1785-1790
9.	Henry James Pye	1790-1813
10.	Robert Southey	1813-1843
11.	William Wordsworth	1843-1850
12.	Alfred, Lord Tennyson	1850-1892
13.	Alfred Austin	1896-1913
14.	Robert Bridges	1913-1930
15.	John Masefield	1930-1967
16.	C. Day Lewis	1967-1972
17.	Sir John Betjeman	1972-1984
18.	Ted Hughes	1984-1998
19.	Andrew Motion	1999- 2009
20.	Carol Ann Duffy	2009-2019
21.	Simon Armitage	from May 2019 onwards

Brief Overview of other Literary Awards and Prizes

National Book Award: presented every November in the United States.

Women's Prize for Fiction: Founded in 1996, the Prize was known by several names viz., Orange Prize for Fiction (1996-2006 and 2009-2012), Orange Broad Band Prize for Fiction (2007-2008) and Bailey's Women's Prize for Fiction (2014-2017) is one of the most prominent literary prizes in the UK. Presented annually and the recipient is a female author of any country. It's given to the finest original full-length novel written in English and published in the UK the previous year.

PEN American Literary Award: The PEN America Literary Awards recognise excellent writers in fiction, poetry, theatre, science and sports writing, essays, biography, and children's literature. Each year, PEN America bestows over 20 honours, fellowships, grants, and prizes totaling almost $350,000 on writers and translators.

HINDU Literary Prize: Also known as The Hindu Best Fiction Award, was founded in 2010 by The Hindu Literary Review, which is part of the daily The Hindu. It recognises Indian writings in English and translations into English. The prize was first named The Hindu Best Fiction Award in 2010. Beginning in 2018, a non-fiction category was added.

Neustadt International Prize for Literature: The University of Oklahoma and its worldwide literary newspaper, World Literature Today, sponsor the Neustadt International Prize for Literature on a biennial basis. It is regarded as one of the most prominent worldwide literary awards, frequently compared to the Nobel Prize in Literature. In 1982, the New York Times dubbed the award "The Oklahoma Nobel," and it is also known as the "American Nobel." Since its inception in 1970, 30 of its laureates, contenders, or jurors have also received Nobel Prizes. It, like the Nobel Prize, is given to individuals for their complete body of work rather than a single one.

The Hugo Award: The most prestigious award given to writers of science fiction. Since 1953, members of the World Science Fiction Convention have gathered annually to vote and administer the awards.

John Newbery Medal: Established in 1922, the John Newbery Medal is awarded by the Association for Library Service to Children to authors of "the most distinguished contribution to American literature for children."

Edgar Award:

The leading organisation for mystery authors, industry professionals involved in the crime writing industry, aspiring crime authors, and fans of the genre is called Mystery Writers of America. The MWA is committed to elevating the status of the genre of crime writing as well as recognising and honouring its authors. This honour is given by Mystery Writers of America each spring.

WORKS CITED

Adler, Thomas P. *Mirror on the Stage: The Pulitzer Plays as an Approach to American Drama*. Purdue University Press, 1989.

"Consultants and Poets Laureate: Poet Laureate: Poetry & Literature: Programs: Library of Congress." *The Library of Congress*,   www.loc.gov/programs/poetry-and-literature/poet-laureate/poets-laureate/. Accessed 7 June. 2023.

"FAQ." *The Sinclair Lewis Society: FAQ*, english.illinoisstate.edu/sinclairlewis/sinclair_lewis/faq/faq2.shtml. Accessed 6 Sept. 2023.

Fischer, Heinz Dietrich, and Erika J. Fischer. *Chronicle of The Pulitzer Prizes for Poetry Discussions, Decisions and Documents*. K G Saur, 2009.

Fischer, Heinz Dietrich, and Erika J. Fischer. *Chronicle of The Pulitzer Prizes for Fiction Discussions, Decisions, and Documents*. K.G. Saur, 2012.

"International Booker Prize." Wikipedia, Wikimedia Foundation, 8 Aug. 2023, en.wikipedia.org/wiki/International_Booker_Prize. Accessed 15 Aug. 2023.

"List of Nobel Laureates in Literature." Wikipedia, Wikimedia Foundation, 23 Aug. 2023, en.wikipedia.org/wiki/List_of_Nobel_laureates_in_Literature.

"Moortidevi Award." Wikipedia, Wikimedia Foundation, 24 Feb. 2023, en.wikipedia.org/wiki/Moortidevi_Award. Accessed 15 Aug. 2023.

"Nobel Prize." Wikipedia, Wikimedia Foundation, 25 Aug. 2023, en.wikipedia.org/wiki/Nobel_Prize. Accessed 15 Aug. 2023.

9 7 9 8 8 9 1 3 3 4 1 8 2